by Ravi Fraps
illustrated by Nicole Wong

Target Skill Consonant *Rr*/r/
High-Frequency Words *me, with, she*

PEARSON
Scott
Foresman

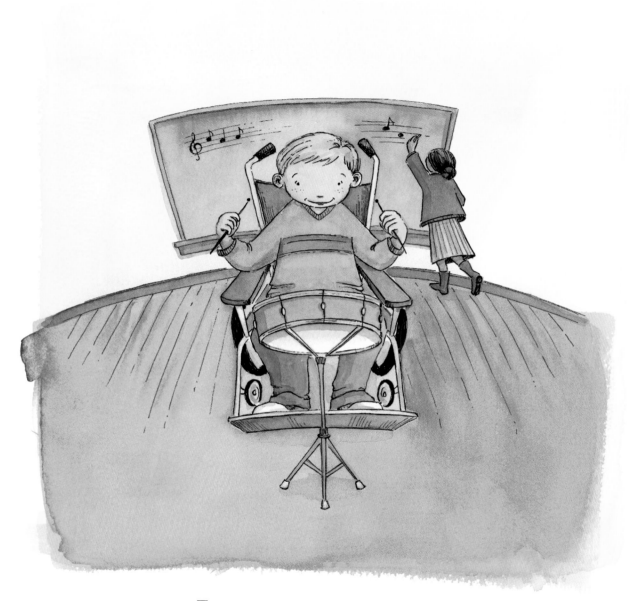

I can tap.

Tap, tap, tap!

Pam can rap.

Rap, rap, rap!

Rin can bam.

Bam, bam, bam!

Pam likes to rap with me.

She can rap, rap, rap.

Rin likes to bam with me.
She can bam, bam, bam.

We can tap, rap, bam.

Tap, rap, bam!

Tap, rap, bam!

We like to tap, rap, bam.

Tap, rap, bam!

Tap, rap, bam!